IRIS APFEL

Fascinating Facts About A Fashion Icon

Index

1

Introduction

In the realm of fashion, individuality is crucial. In terms of improving your confidence as a woman, the way you appear, express yourself, perceive yourself, and appreciate yourself makes a huge difference. Iris Apfel is known for influencing many younger women, and women generally, in the worlds of fashion and style, especially when it comes to self-confidence and looks. Her style is all about personality.

She instilled confidence in countless women, changing their lives completely. She enabled every woman she met to look exactly how they wanted to, without making them look ridiculous or cultivating an ambition to be like other women, but rather to enjoy and enhance their appearance. After meeting Apfel or seeing one of her shows, they do realize that they no longer had to dress or behave like everyone else.

Apfel makes you aware that your attire tells us a lot about your personality and that your clothes may also transfer and influence your personality. At 100 years old and still a style icon, her symbolism says much about her style. Individual freedom and modernism are embodied by the fashion, interiors, and textile legend Iris Apfel.

I had never considered myself as being pretty, as she would remark. I'm not always in the mood to feel so. I'm not particularly attractive. Pretty does not appeal to me. Though I don't' feel horrible either. And I believe it panned off beautifully since I discovered that all the girls, I knew who got by on beautiful attractiveness faded over time and became nothing. And they were quite dissatisfied. Once you're someone such as I am, then you will need to produce something, study something, and accomplish something to get around and be appealing. As a result, you become much more intriguing.

Iris Apfel, a New York American with a sinister personal style, is someone you should know. She's the best-looking high fashionista in the world, and with years of professional experience under her belt, she's got the sage advice of an intelligent old owl.

With her personality, quotations, and how she interprets everyday life, this trendsetter has inspired not only the world of fashion but the rest of the globe. With vibrancy and quips as distinctive as her accouterments and signature eyeglasses, the 'Geriatric Starlet' recounts her life of high style.

This Book has some wonderful zingers and insights that will benefit both your sense of fashion and your whole lifestyle. It'll be an intriguing journey throughout. So, buckle up as we take this journey alongside.

2

Iris Apfel's childhood

Learn more about Iris Apfel. Who is Iris Apfel, truly? Sadye and Samuel Barrel's only child, Iris Apfel, acquired her parents' influence—wit, assertiveness, the enthusiasm for adventure, and, obviously, their flair for fashion. Her parents drew a huge amount of interest, especially her mom, who had a high degree of distinctive appearance and defied traditional gender roles as the founder of a clothes business for many years. But on the other hand, Apfel's father was an industrialist who established a mirror and glassware company.

Since Iris Apfel was her parent's only child, her parents frequently took her to family gatherings where she was almost the only child there. Apfel's grandma entertained her by letting her explore fabric trimmings, which she had in abundance since her 4 children frequently stitched for philanthropy. These materials nurtured her interest in fashion and apparel, which has rubbed off on her health and lifestyle. The variety of colors, designs, and sensations within those fabric remnants delighted her. This sparked her interest in fashion. This occurred in the nineties when she was about eleven years of age.

Usually, if Apfel had handled the situation well, her grandma would let her take home six pieces after each visit. This caused her to become infatuated with texture, color, and design, and she dedicated her evenings to doing so, which piqued her fascination more with textiles.

Oh, and I almost failed to add that this renowned figure, Iris Apfel was brought into the world on August 29, 1921, in Queens, New York. She completed her study at New York University and the University of Wisconsin, where she majored in art history. She began working for the Women's Wear Daily fashion magazine after finishing her schooling. She is the daughter of a glassware and mirror company owner and a Russian-born mom who runs a fashion store.

How and why did Iris Apfel become a fashion icon?

I believe the term "influence" is the appropriate answer to this question. Influence is the ability to inspire decisions, to persuade or compel them to obtain their acceptance. To be honest, she had no intention of becoming an icon or actively pursuing a life in the fashion world.

Her ambition upon graduating from the University of Wisconsin has been to work in the fashion profession as a writer. She took an entry-level job at Women's Wear Daily in Manhattan before moving on to designer Robert Goodman. This was how she met Elinor Johnson, an interior designer who recruited her because of her excellent sense of design and thus began her interior decorating career.

Given the constraints imposed by World War II on businesses that depended on shipping from Europe, there was plenty of room for different innovative designs to be developed domestically. This was where she got most of her opportunity to innovate her designs.

Apfel is now known for her diverse aesthetic. She wears combinations of saturated colors, big spectacles, and accessories with such panache that she was the centerpiece of a show at The Metropolitan Museum of Art's Costume Institute between September 13, 2005, to January 22, 2006.

Interestingly, Apfel was 84 years old when the show first started. She is now amongst the liveliest figures in the fields of style, fabrics, and interior decorating, and she has developed a funny and extravagantly unique individual style well over the past several decades. "She is known for blending high and low styles, such as Dior haute couture with flea market finds, and 19th-century church trappings with Dolce & Gabbana lizard slacks."

Apfel has also achieved widespread celebrity, having recently been transformed into a one-of-a-kind Blow-up doll that was launched in conjunction with Apfel's journal. With her unique style sense, business ambition, and assertiveness, Iris Apfel is the ultimate Barbie model citizen. Her extensive profession gives her the ideal topic for a one-of-a-kind doll, Barbie's ultimate distinction.

Even the name "geriatric starlet" was assigned by Apfel herself. She founded and managed Old-World Weavers, a multinational textile production company, alongside her husband, Carl Apfel, who were freshly married at the time.

Old World Weavers was operated by the husband-and-wife team until 1992, and during that period, they worked for nine White House administrations, from Harry Truman to Bill Clinton. According to her book, Apfel earned the nickname "First Lady of Fabric" or "Our Lady of the Cloth" during her service at the White House.

Because the Apfel couldn't find fabrics in the United States, they would fly to Europe twice a year to obtain textiles. They saw this as a great chance to focus on fabric productions from the 17th through the 19th century, and they opened a storefront at 115 East 57th Avenue in New York City, New York.

"At the age of ninety, she got her first large job in the fashion and beauty industry. For the winter of 2011, she created a limited-edition makeup line for MAC cosmetic products. As a result, she is the longest-living actress to ever appear in a prominent cosmetic product commercial.

Apfel's brand launched on the Home Shopping Network in 2011. "Rara Avis" is the name of the brand, which comprises a variety of huge, bright accessories.

Apfel's life was chronicled in a docudrama broadcast in 2014. It was produced by Albert Maysles, the renowned documentary director, and was shortlisted for an Award nomination in 2017, known Emmy.

An ensemble isn't fully functional without a distinctive piece, or several, to showcase your originality, she'd say.

Glasses are my thing, and the wider and clearer, the more love I have for them. To create an eyeglasses collection, I realized I needed to locate a fantastic eyeglasses collaborator.

Permit me to recap again that Iris Apfel is a style icon around the world. She is still going strong even at the age of 100.

What drives this legend to make the best of life at such a young age?

She had always demonstrated that age is only a number. Notwithstanding her advanced years, she remains 'vertical as vibrant as ever.

3

Philosophy of Apfel

I'm confident that some people are uninterested in fashion. Even if you aren't interested in colorful, bold fashion, Apfel's words of wisdom on aging, individualism, self-esteem, attractiveness, and success are worth reading after nearly a century on the earth.

Her philosophy of life could motivate us. What I mean by "philosophy of life" is a conceptual paradigm for comprehending how the world functions and how you integrate into it. Issues such as how you determine what is "desirable" and "terrible," what "accomplishments" means, what your "mission" in life is, including if you don't believe there is one if there is indeed a God, how we ought to treat one another, and so on would be covered as a philosophical outlook. It can also refer to any broad viewpoint on the meaning and purpose of living or how one should live one's life. The phrase also focuses on a particular manner of thinking about philosophical musings.

Envision those who have lived ten decades and yet are still flourishing in their profession at the age of 100. Her philosophy is necessary to discuss. When I'm done sharing her philosophy with you, she'll be such an inspiration to you.

1. Don't get caught up in your age

"I rarely worry about my age," she stated. Perhaps that's the key. It's never crossed my mind; it's a fleeting thought. It's only a number… Work is beneficial to my health. I am passionate about what I am doing and give it my all. So, I hardly think or worry about my age.

"Growing old is just not for sissies," Apfel acknowledges. So, what now? "You begin to fall away, but all you have to do now is get back up and glue yourself back on." You may not enjoy growing older, but what do you have to lose? You've arrived at that age. Accept it. I recommend putting your expertise to good use by helping others."

In contemporary civilization, there are a plethora of unpleasant misconceptions regarding aging. This may make many of us (both men and women) fear growing elderly, yet there are numerous significant advantages to growing older that we tend to overlook. Just continue to read, and I'll discuss some with you soon.

Take, for example, grandkids. You'll get to enjoy the benefits of having youngsters without the responsibility and expectations that come with parenthood. And the affection you offer and experience from your grandkids is a win-win situation for both of you. That's one of several advantages of becoming older. Continue reading to learn about a few more.

Iris Apfel never advised you not to marry. Her stance was significant, and I admire it. She made a responsible choice, albeit a tough one for other women.

There are numerous advantages to growing older. Another is being overwhelmed by joy. According to studies, aging mothers are among the healthiest individuals on the planet, particularly in comparison to their middle-aged contemporaries. This could be due to improved effective coping strategies or interesting to note that elderly individuals are increasingly at ease in their very own skin. In any event, as we become elderly, enhanced contentment and tranquility are surely something there to look ahead to.

You'll have extra free time, which is another huge advantage. When you resign, you'll not only possess more time to spend with your friends and family, but you'll also have additional opportunities to do new things.

Jim Stack, a Clare resident, proves that it isn't too late to change it up a bit. He withdrew from work and started sketching and painting, and anyone could do the same, no matter how old they were or even what personal circumstances they had.

After that, there's Unlimited Intelligence

Age brings a wealth of lessons and knowledge. According to one study, aging moms had higher compassionate and oriented communication, as well as increased psychological management. People in their 60s and far beyond have a greater range of viewpoints, conclusions, and agreements than those in their 20s and 30s.

Financial Gains

Some monetary benefits come with being older. Aging mothers have assured healthcare coverage and a national minimum wage because of programs like Medicare, Medicaid, and Welfare Benefits. Retirement reductions are, of course, a fantastic benefit of becoming elderly. They not only allow the elderly to experience life and stay involved and healthy, but they also allow them to conserve money when their revenue is regulated and constrained.

The advantages of growing older are endless. It's up to you to seek them out and capitalize on them. Iris Apfel made use of the information provided here. She grew old gracefully. Among the many things reported about her, one that stands out is that she was allegedly the very first woman to adopt a pair of trousers.

That would be just one among a million pleasures that this magnificence has to offer.

Iris Apfel is one of the liveliest figures in the fields of style, fabric, and interior decorating, and she has developed a funny and extravagantly unique individual taste over the past 40 years. At the age of 100, she seems to have become an "Unintentional Icon" with nearly 2 million Instagram admirers, according to her admission.

On the inside, there is beauty. Her personality continues to provide her satisfaction. The late Albert Maysles' video "Iris" captures her never-ending joy. He captures her in a variety of fashion events, where she is both unconventional and stylish.

2. Find a companion who congratulates you on your accomplishments

This is crucial. It is not necessary to have an ostentatious gathering or give an exorbitant present to celebrate yourself or your accomplishments.

There are numerous ways to cultivate this routine that are simple to include in your daily routine.

Some easy methods to celebrate include keeping a victory diary, devoting a whole day to treating yourself, or having a meal with friends and family. Perhaps all you need to celebrate is a day spent doing anything you enjoy but don't usually have the opportunity to do.

You have an excellent incentive to justify a party whenever you achieve those goals. You've made a lot of sacrifices and faced challenges along the road for every significant accomplishment in your life, and it's crucial to recognize and celebrate those unique victories.

Apfel hailed her late husband for this act by saying, "Everyone he ever touched knows he was genuinely a Gentle Man," Apfel wrote about Carl.

His compassion and wit were renowned. We accomplished collaboratively almost everything we had. His unfailing words of encouragement enabled me to attain my goals. He thrust me into the spotlight before basking in my glory. He was far more amused than I was by the compliments I earned from him. I adore him. "Good night, beautiful soul, My Prince."

3. Go for it when something interests you

This was one of Apfel's major points. When you are excited about doing something, if it allows you to feel glad, enthusiastic, or motivated, then go for it. The most essential benefit of enthusiasm is that it is communicable, which means that when you are enthusiastic, you motivate individuals even without their knowledge. Enthusiasm generates more focus and flare. This will hasten your progress toward success.

It can also assist you in overcoming challenges. When you're enthusiastic about something, you see difficulties differently and come up with creative solutions. Enthusiasm can divert your attention away from difficulties for a short time, allowing you to think more critically and come up with something better and transforming.

Simultaneously, enthusiasm enhances enjoyment. People possess greater vigor and are healthier emotionally when they are enthusiastic.

"I rarely anticipated people knowing my name or identifying my appearance," Apfel added. I never saw myself as a fashionista. My apparel accouterments were never supposed to be displayed in museums. In my nineties, I never imagined being a magazine girl or the brand of a beauty firm. I just do what my instinct tells me to do. I do things because they appear thrilling and fascinating, and then I agonize about them subsequently. It requires tremendous passion and courage to try out and explore something different. Making events happen, learning how to perfect trade, and pushing worries aside can be exhausting.

It's so much harder for most folks to just go with the trend. However, it's not particularly fascinating."

4. "You have to think young to stay young"

"As you become aged, as an old family friend used to say, if you have twice of something, some of them is bound to ache once you get up early in the morning."

But you must get up and move past the discomfort. You must feel youthful if you desire to look sharp and stay young. "My elixirs are a feeling of astonishment, a sense of amusement, and a sense of inquiry," she explains. "They preserve you youthful and playful, try getting adaptable to different types of experiences, and be eager for the next experience."

I'll not become an aged fuddy-duddy; I'm the World's Oldest Living Teenager, and I aim to maintain this status quo as long as I live."

This is exactly accurate: you are as old as you believe. It's simple to calculate biological maturity. You may find out how many decades, years, or months have passed since your birthday anniversary by counting how many decades, months, or weeks have passed since your birthdate by counting how many years, months, or days have passed since your birthday counting how many years, months since it encompasses intelligence, recollection, linguistic information processing, and other characteristics, brain age is somewhat more sophisticated.

Fitness level is also important since if you are in good form and don't have many complaints and problems, you may appear to be more youthful than you are. While someone may be 70 years old technically, they may still be cognitively and generally fit, yet they appear to be in their middle age.

Psychological maturity refers to how old you believe you are rather than how old you are based on factual factors such as how long you've been living or how well you do on cognitive tests. In a logical sequence, everybody matures, but cognitive aging is a unique thing altogether. A group of investigators discovered a link between the psychological age that an older person experiences and their scientifically highly reliable maturity in a recent study published in Frontiers Neuroscience. Specifically, if you feel younger than your age, your brain age is likely to reflect that with improved cognitive and memory skills. Physical disease, exercise performance, and other things, on the other hand, can make someone feel times older than they are.

It's one thing to have a subjective perspective of being 40 when you're 70, but is there a verifiable variation in learning and memory? Dr. Jeanyung Chey of Seoul National University in Korea sought to study this subject. Dr. Chey inquires, "The reason why some persons appear to be younger or older than they are. Emotional conditions, psychological characteristics, and physical functioning are all considerations. However, no one had looked at cognitive aging pathways as a probable cause of perceived age disparities."

There are indicators for brain age, and researchers can correctly estimate brain age using high-tech neuroimaging. Apart from minor cognitive or speech comprehension impairments, we lose grey matter as we age. This is where the study team concentrated their research. Dr. Gray and her colleagues at SNU studied 68 healthy individuals ranging in age from 59 to 84 years old. The amount of grey matter in various parts of the brain was examined, and intellectual testing was performed. Respondents were requested about how old they felt and whether their subjective age was younger or older than their real age. Those who said they felt younger than their age performed better on cognitive tests, were physically healthier, and were less depressed. The fact that those who felt younger than they had more grey matter in important brain regions than those who felt older was the most noteworthy finding.

According to Dr. Chey, "People who feel younger have the anatomical traits of a younger brain, according to our findings. Importantly, even when other plausible characteristics such as personality, subjective health, depressive symptoms, or cognitive functions are taken into consideration, the difference persists." It's unclear if people who feel older can detect brain changes that reflect aging. It's also likely that individuals who feel younger naturally gravitate toward a more active lifestyle that involves exercise and socialization, both of which can assist older adults in keeping their minds and bodies sharp. The authors also recommend that if a person feels older than they are, they examine their food habits and lifestyle adjustments rather than simply accepting their age and lack of fitness.

I don't consider myself to be elderly, and I prefer not to. I feel young on the inside, and I'd like to keep feeling that way. Obviously, I've grown older when I look in the mirror, but I don't usually feel old; instead, I feel young.

5. Prioritize your viewpoint over that of others

Some might even refer to it as "having compassion for yourself." for you, it's safe. If you give quite so much credence to what people say, you risk ruining your reputation. You can become a negative attribute to yourself by caring as much about whatever others perceive about you.

You get into difficulty when you begin to concentrate on what other individuals consider of you and make their judgment crucial to your achievement. From that point forward, you begin adapting your life to meet the demands of others, and this trend continues.

We neglect the importance of who we are once we hand over our control to others and accept their perceptions to shape who we are. We can only perceive ourselves as we assume others view us.

"I don't ever attempt to blend in," Iris Apfel explains. It's not that I set out to be such a rebel or do kinds of stuff that were morally reprehensible — I did, after all, have to learn how to play bridge when I was younger — but I understood early on that I needed to be my person to be happy.

"If you try to be everything to everyone, you'll wind up being 'nothing' to no one." Those who sense such a need to identify the style of how I dress or what I wear may be 'strange' or 'eccentric,' but that doesn't bother me. I don't use my outfit to attract attention; I dress to express myself. You don't have to think like every other person if you don't dress the same as everyone else."

You got to know where you're headed or even what the fact is; you do not have to be what others want you to be. You're entitled to be whoever you choose to be." Be who you choose to be and appreciate everything your heart perceives.

It's crucial to recognize what makes you unique to figure out who you want to be. Transformation is the technique of understanding what keeps you unique, and it is an important component of personality. Everyone has amazing traits and capabilities that set them apart from their peers. Do what your heart cries out for to minimize possibly poisonous interference and pressures from those around you.

Determine what brings you joy. Consider all or most of the elements that afford joy. Compile a checklist of all the things you like to do every day. Furthermore, consider why these activities bring joy. You might understand what makes you miserable by figuring out what makes you happy. Once you've figured out what brings you joy, consider devoting greater attention to those pursuits.

Begin to love yourself as though you were a totally different personality. Remind yourself of what makes you a fantastic individual daily. You can accomplish this by admiring yourself and your abilities or sending yourself encouraging messages. Higher levels of optimism contribute to increased self-confidence and consciousness, as well as a greater sense of contentment with your own unique identity. You are what you define yourself to be. More than anyone else's voice, amplify your own voice about yourself.

6. However, do not isolate yourself

To paraphrase the poet of Mr. John Donne, I am aware that I am not an island but rather a portion of the mainland. I fit in, yet in my unique manner. I've never been much of a traditionalist in any way, and it hasn't injured me yet in my ninety-plus years, so I seem to be accomplishing something properly... But then, if you refuse to strive to participate, you'll be forgotten, and that's when your uniqueness will work against you. First, get in, then get out. There is a distinction between being seen as unique and being embraced, even adored for it, and being seen as unique and being despised for that though. It's possible you eat your cake and still have your cake."

To be isolated sometimes has its advantages. There are, obviously, certain disadvantages likewise. Being alone yourself can help you be more productive and creative.

Enquire from any innovative rationalist: settling quietly and generating concepts on one 's own is frequently the greatest effective approach. By turning off the outside noises, you can become more in tune with your thinking, allowing your mind to roam while also allowing your intellectual energy to flourish. So, no matter how quick a decision-maker you are, you'll need some solitary chance to ponder it over. Being by ourselves allows our intellect to rejuvenate. Making friends and interacting with people is always essential to optimal cognitive function but switching off your head occasionally is also beneficial — all it's about finding the right balance.

You can cleanse your mind by making any assumptions, functioning more effectively in an uncluttered environment with no disturbances. Just remember to eat healthily and get enough rest during the process.

Relationships Can Benefit from Being Alone

Private time from our spouses, realize it or otherwise, can be beneficial. Separation for these little moments enables you to reclaim a sense of autonomy that you may not have had in years while also establishing a better attitude of admiration for your respective partner. It's healthy to appreciate folks, particularly when a personal reconnection is imminent.

Being Alone, on the other hand, can keep you depressed

You've probably heard the phrase "don't let your thoughts go soft." Indolence, on the other hand, can have the same effect. Not figuratively, but you must engage with literature, crossword, or just any reasonable job regularly to keep your brain performing at its best. Spending Too Much Time Alone Would be Harmful to Your Psychological Wellness

There is a distinction to be made between being solitary and being lonesome. And, as you might expect, too much of the first can start to resemble the other. It's crucial to distinguish the number of hours spent all alone and your feelings about that time. Loneliness can cause not only mental but also bodily distress. So, make use of modern television services or messaging apps to communicate and share information.

It's Possible to Become Depressed When You're Alone. Isolation and sadness have long been linked; certain investigations have even revealed morphological changes between a "normal" brain and one starving for contact. Too much seclusion produces mental swings, prompting patients to have an unfavorable perception of the world around them. Telemedicine facilities and helplines can assist folks who are suffering signs of depressive episodes that are more severe than usual.

Taking some time for oneself usually has no negative consequences. However, we are currently living in a moment that can hardly be regarded as normal. When seclusion is a government-mandated need, confining your thoughts and physique while indoors isn't really.

7. You can't purchase success with money

"A success is being pleased, starting a relationship, being around fantastic people, pursuing what you enjoy, and giving something back to the society." "Dedicating your life for the dollar isn't worth the significant cost - at least not so much to me," Apfel says.

8. It is not about wasting money to be stylish

"Fashion isn't about dressing up in high fashion. You could possess a huge amount of riches but no sense of fashion. She writes, "You can be adorned in the newest design, outfitted in ten-thousand-dollar footwear, and be bauble to the nines, and yet look like a Christmas tree." "What matters is how you wear it, not really what you are wearing, even as this matter." I'm just as delighted to wear three-dollar bracelets as I am to wear expensive items, and I enjoy mixing high and low, trying to put things together to wear as the mood strikes me. When you strive too much to be stylish, you come across as uneasy, as if you're dressed up, and the outfits are approaching the house without you.

You won't be capable of pulling off even the most ideal look when you're stressed. If this is the case, I recommend abandoning the project entirely. It is preferable to be joyful with your style and design than well dressed."

9. Begin new projects with a tiny step

"You only fail if you never give it an attempt," Apfel explains. Yes, you've failed if you give up without trials. When we strive to achieve something unusual, we frequently stumble and occasionally fail. But smile, because the more you do something like this, the more expert you will become at it.

If everything that does not go according to plan is viewed as a failure, you will never truly understand what victory is. You may also lack the strength to try confronting the numerous trials required to achieve excellence. You won't feel confident enough to try new things. You will never understand the actual delight that comes from confronting and conquering your anxieties and hardships.

"I never thought I couldn't achieve something because I was a woman," Iris Apfel stated. I'd always wanted to start a fabric company, so I just did it. I definitely would not have achieved my ambition if I had given too much thought to establish Old World Weavers. It's sometimes necessary to simply act immediately, even if it's a modest effort.

In my ninety years on this world, I've devoted considerable effort to living — and looking my way — and it's never led me astray."

Essentially, it boils down to this: don't be scared of failure. Things are certain to go awry. Your attitude on life is determined by how you choose to view your difficulties. You will become highly knowledgeable and finally prosperous if you view challenges as training materials.

10. Don't act younger than you are

"Wrinkles are very normal." Attempting to seem much more youthful when you're elderly is pointless, and you're not deceiving anybody. Nobody will believe you're thirty if you have a makeover at the age of eighty. Just embrace what you have. Make your age inconsequential.

4

Apfel Jewelry Journey

I f there's one thing Apfel's birthplace of New York can be commended for, it's that the city appreciates elegance. As previously stated, Apfel was born in Queens in 1921. She was born to two Jewish farmers. Apfel began traveling the subway to Manhattan when she was 12 years old to explore local vintage merchants. This was how h Her extensive jewelry collection began.

"She could travel the entire mass transit system for a nickel at the time, so she would visit a new part of New York every week—Chinatown, Yorkville, Harlem, Greenwich Square." And she was completely smitten by the Villages. "I started poking around large retail stores in the Village and became fascinated with all this ancient crap," she explained.

Iris Apfel is currently as busy as always, jet-setting among fashion exhibitions and photo sessions and collaborating on high-profile fashion projects.

The jewelry was discovered during Iris' travels over the years—she and her husband, Carl, established the renowned textiles firm Old-World Weavers, which took her to all parts of the planet and allowed her to deal with everyone from Dorothy Draper to the Kennedys—and "is fantastic motivational sayings."

Everything changed for Apfel in 2005 when the Costume Institute of The Metropolitan Museum of Art opted to feature her in a show called Rara Avis: Pieces from the Iris Apfel Museum. The originally intended display had been postponed, and the designer, Harold Koda, had an epiphany and decided to approach Apfel about her famed handmade jewelry collection.

Apfel's jewelry, fantasy clothing, and iconic tortoiseshell glasses were highlighted in the subsequent presentation. "An American innovative in the purest sense of the word, Iris Apfel is among the most ebullient personality types in the worlds of fashion, fabrics, and interior decorating, and over the past 40 years, she has fostered a unique preference that is both humorous and extravagantly iconoclastic," this the museum wrote of her eclectic style.

Apfel's signature look, which included round glasses, pieces of jewelry, and patterned clothing, made her a well-known personality in the fashion world. Her style quickly became a go-to for Halloween outfits and costume parties. Her fashion advice went viral on the Internet. Mattel honored Apfel with a Barbie doll in 2018, the brand's highest award.

After Tommy Hilfiger's support, she received a supermodel deal with IMG in 2019. Since then, Apfel has starred in a slew of commercials and commercial collaborations. She most recently published The Iris Apfel Centennial Collection with Zenni Optical five days before her 100th birthday. The capsule assortment is a five-frame eyeglasses series that reflects Apfel's unique accessories concept.

"An ensemble isn't complete without a distinctive accessory, or several trademark accessories, to showcase your originality." "The lot brighter the eyeglasses, the better," she explained.

Age is just a number, as the adage goes. Late-life is, nevertheless, Apfel's best accessory to date, thanks to the way she wears it. She believes that jewelry is the most transformational of all accouterments. You may move from day to night by simply altering the accessories you choose with a beautiful black gown. If money was tight, my mother advised me to invest in a few well-cut staples and add flair with accessories. You personalize them and make them your own with the accessories you choose. This is wisdom from the Great Depression, yet it still holds today. Bangles that look great with an expensive couture outfit can be found at flea markets. People will tell you that you can't just go out and get some rubbish and combine it with something so valuable. But I enjoy doing it.

5

Apfel's marriage

Iris Apfel is a fashion icon which is both fascinating and unconventional. As a result, she was one of the last subjects of cinematographer Albert Maysles, who died earlier this year after finishing a film about the New York fashion guru's profession, lifestyle, and beautiful romance.

Iris displays her glamorous lifestyle, complete with gigantic bracelets and pendants, fuzzy shawls, multi-colored gowns, and, of course, her distinctive spherical-shape eyeglasses. That's the kind of thing she likes to dress up in.

On Independence Day, they went out for the first time. Carl had suggested the Festive season. I received a blinged this Christmas. "We were wedded on Washington's anniversary."

Carl Apfel married Iris on February 22, 1948. She selected a bright pink wedding gown since it can be re-worn, despite her independence in fashion and pragmatic character.

Her option not to raise children was much more private. Apfel refused to identify as a feminist, but she did reject the lifestyle that was required of her as a woman in the mid-twentieth century. She chose to concentrate on her work and a lifestyle of exploring the world alongside her hubby alternatively.

Apfel has long defied gender norms. Apfel persisted in acquiring a pair of trousers to complement an appearance she had envisioned in an age where women were required to wear "feminine" clothes. She maintains a passionate mentality of tolerance regarding maturing in a contemporary generation, which drives women to retain an image of youth. Apfel feels that women should not change their outward appearance in an attempt to pretend to be younger than they are, and she embraces her age. She also blends designer and low-cost, popular items, bridging the gap between "haute couture" and "cheap" or "affordable" labels.

Iris arranged a birthday celebration for Carl on his 100th anniversary, inviting everyone else from Ruben and Isabel Toledo to Linda Fargo of Bergdorf Goodman and artist Naeem Khan.

Iris and Carl initially managed to meet in 1947 while vacationing at a lodge on Lake George in upstate New York for an appointment interview with The Guardian.

Both became immediately drawn to one another upon discussing. "There was just something with Iris that just went inside my heart," Carl stated in the video about Iris. It is constantly present." After hearing what Carl had to say, Iris concluded, "I realized he was nice, adorable, and served Chinese, so I couldn't do anymore."

In a video, Iris stated that she had intended to abscond rather than marry, but her relatives insisted on marriage. "I would prefer to get the cash," Iris explained, "but our family and grandparents desired the marriage...

My wedding was modest—just about 125 individuals were present; it was quite fancy."

Iris didn't manage to run away as intended, but she did receive a great deal on the bridal gown of her fantasies.

"The gown was a pink silk, and I'm quite utilitarian," Iris noted, "so I chose a gown that I could enjoy after the wedding and not put in a closet after my wedding." She continued, "I still possess that footwear for 66 and a half years now." "They resembled a pale pink satin," she explained. They've come back into fashion. Everything eventually returns if you stick around hard enough."

After two years as a wedded pair, the pair co-founded Old World Weavers, a textile firm that repairs household items and designs. "We initially did not expect us to go into the clothing industry," Iris said after starting the clothing industry. Hardly anything I've ever done was on purpose. It just all sort of fell into place."

Carl and Iris collaborated on several initiatives simultaneously, including that of the White House and the Museum of Modern Art. They also went on travels to Turkey, Morocco, and Lebanon to acquire everything, including haute couture items to knickknacks once per design to delight her clientele and leave them pleased.

Please allow me to describe exactly how these couples interacted.

"We were on the same page." Moreover, as Iris pointed out, a positive mindset was crucial "There was a sensation of excitement and respect for each other, and I wasn't expecting him to like most of my pals, but he didn't – which was generally fine. We didn't always have to do everything simultaneously. We did practically everything around each other, except when he was into sports, and I was not.

One of several best aspects of tying the knot was that I didn't have to attend any sporting events. 'Wouldn't go to a game since he potentially could go,' I never warned him. There were some activities that he disliked that I always adore, likewise."

6

Does Apfel have children?

Aptel is an entrepreneur, creative and innovative professional, and fashion model from the United States. She ran a textile manufacturing company with her hubby, Carl, from 1950 to 1992, along with an agreement with the White House that lasted nine presidents. She received recognition for a 2005 exhibition at The Metropolitan Museum of Art's Costume Institute, which featured her assortment of fashion accessories staged on mannequins as she would wear them. She has now become a fashion designer, signing with IMG in 2019 as a model at the age of 97 and being included in Albert Maysles' 2014 video Iris.

The Apfels never had offspring, partially considering the extent of how they travel, as required by their jobs, and mainly because she didn't really want h to be reared by a babysitter, which may hamper a healthy growing time.

Her decisions in life:

"I rarely desired a baby, and I didn't have any. You can't have it all, and I always knew that I wanted to work, "she stated.

The nonagenarian fashion maestro still has the will to accomplish more at this age of her life. She mentioned a future collaboration with American chain store Neiman Marcus in a Q&A with Tank magazine's editor Caroline Issa, as well as a novel she "desires to finish" that "won't be pricey" and is targeted at a "younger demographic."

7

Iris Apfel fascinating facts and philosophy

Iris Apfel believes that dressing comfortably is important, but she also believes in dressing modestly. She feels our current attires are "too comfy" sometimes. While being comfortable is important, Apfel advises against appearing too relaxed. "Some exploit the opportunity and begin to look unkempt," she told The Talks. Baggy sweatshirts, according to Apfel, should only ever be used in recreational contexts – rarely at the cinema, for example. The theatre used to have a black-tie proper attire, as she told The New Potato. "Now you're sitting beside somebody wearing tattered t-shirts and soiled jeans," she explained. "That isn't correct."

Feeling more relaxed and looking confident, according to Apfel, are two different things. She has had a major influence in the modeling industry as a trendsetter for generations. Her private experience has also been quite interesting.

Iris Apfel believes that excellent design is all about pleasure.

One of the components of quality design, according to Iris, is a pleasure. "You can't look attractive if you're not relaxed and happy," she explained. She continued, saying, "You should not be wearing your garments if they don't give you pleasure. You must dress appropriately." Many people believe that beautiful fashion isn't necessarily pleasant, but Iris Apfel believes otherwise.

Pleasure is the goal of style. When clothing is excessively restrictive or seems unusual on the physique, according to Apfel, it's usually a warning that the fashion isn't right for you and that you'll appear uncomfortable and weird. It affects your mind.

Apfel follows her own advice. She claimed in an appearance with Fashionista that she always prefers flats to stilettos or heels. In an appearance with The

Talks, she revealed that on informal occasions, she typically chooses moderate, comfy attire.

Iris Apfel feels that being comfortably dressed with pleasure is important, but she also specializes in dressing modestly. She thinks current attire is "too comfy" at times, though.

While also being happy is important to your dress sense, Apfel advises against appearing too relaxed. "She told The Talk show; people take advantage and begin to look unprofessional with their dress sense,". "That isn't correct."

Apfel brought up the present trend for casual wearing in another discussion with StyleCaster.

Once questioned what her biggest frustration was, she calmly said, "It is the way some folks appear nowadays. Their dress sense resembles rag piles on wheels." Apfel believes there is a distinction between feeling and seeming confident.

This is what Iris Apfel does to stay awake.

We, I mean everyone, have quirks, and Iris Apfel's is bubble gum. Her chewing gum addiction has been mentioned in numerous appearances. She is constantly carrying a knapsack.

Chewing gum is a method for her to remain alert, as she stated to The Guardian. After all, she is over 10 decades years old!

This tendency makes being attractive a little difficult. She told The Daily Beast in an interview how she rarely understood what to do about her bubble gum during a business lunch or dinner at a restaurant. "People used to keep them beneath the table in the classroom," she said, and obviously, she no longer has that opportunity.

Apfel's bubble gum addiction stretches to her style. She was noted for wearing a bracelet composed of old plastic, including one with a bubble gum package.

Iris Apfel's signature eyeglasses have been a staple of her style for decades.

It's difficult to picture Iris Apfel without her signature wide, spherical eyeglasses. Now it appears that the fashionable revolutionary has been wearing the very same spectacles for centuries, and it's no surprise because they've formed a hallmark of her distinctive personality. When she first acquired spectacles, she selected the renowned eyeglasses. She told Interview Magazine. "If I'm going to wear eyeglasses, let me wear goggles!" she exclaimed.

She also appears to have acquired intriguing eyeglasses and worn them sans glasses or with different lenses, depending on her certification. She does, however, favor large framing.

'Why are you wearing those huge pixels or glasses?' individuals used to usually question her. "'The larger they are for seeing you,' she'd remark," she explained. It appears that Apfel's eyeglasses, like the whole of her apparel and footwear, have always been properly odd, folks would say!

Iris Apfel is not someone who dresses up day after day.

Even though Iris Apfel is renowned for her impeccable taste in fashion, she does not wear costumes nearly every day. She explained to Vanity Fair that she literally cannot nearly every day. "When I'm at my residence, like right now," she continued, "I typically use a robe." She puts on a piece of trousers if she intends to go outside to run some errands for herself. "I adore elegance and believe it is fantastic; however, it is not my lifestyle," she explained.

She reportedly told Vogue that she dislikes spending overly much time getting things altogether. She wastes "no effort whatsoever," in truth. She just loves to be her at all times. Furthermore, as Apfel admitted to The Zoe Report, "as it's all stitched properly," she often repeats the very same dress multiple times in succession. Apfel appears to be a lot less pragmatic and positioned than we thought!

The renowned designer somehow doesn't expect perfectionism.

Iris Apfel's approach is easily defined as excellence — after all, she has an eye-catching, lavish, and stunning flair that nicely complements her outspoken attitude. Perfection, nevertheless, has never been her goal, as she said to The Talks.

But on the other side, her mom was obsessed with perfectionism. "When she woke up, she appeared as if she'd strolled out from a Chicago Coin bandbox," Apfel remembered. "She was flawless at all times." Her mother's appearance, it seems, was always a talking point.

That kind of unwavering excellence isn't Apfel's intention. She exclaimed, "I always just go with the tide!" Instead of fussing over her clothing, Apfel lets her hair down and plays around with different hues. "My Goodness, I really cannot survive in a regimented environment," she said. Apfel's fashion is mostly about making grand decisions, even if they are a touch sloppy at times.

Iris Apfel was taught to be economical as a child. Apfel rose to prominence as an entrepreneur and design magnate. She wasn't always wealthy, though. She revealed to Vanity Fair how her background in a minimal-income family, even during the Great Recession, instilled in her a lifetime appreciation for the value of saving. "I'm a child of something like the recession," she explained, "so I'm really, extremely pragmatic."

When it comes to trends and fashion, Apfel's affordability implies that she prefers to wear her clothing more frequently. She also gets a huge amount of wear out of her preferred clothes because she re-wears them. Apfel even donned her wedding gown more than once. She explained, "I had a wedding gown made that I could repeatedly use, even after my wedding."

And when it comes to shopping, Apfel is always on the lookout for a good deal. "Well, I'm cheap," she confesses to the proprietor of a clothes store during a bargaining discussion in the video "Iris."

Iris Apfel does not have a Middle Name, have you heard any?

Have you ever been curious about Iris Apfel's middle name? Unfortunately, it appears that the style icon may not possess a middle name at all. "I don't think I had a middle name or nickname," she told StyleCaster in 2018.

Because Apfel lacked a genuine middle name that she was aware of, she decided to invent one. She never seemed to be able to choose just one. She adopted a series of "fancy" middle or nicknames as a child, according to reports.

It appears that Apfel's style of innovation isn't the only outlet for her inventiveness.

Nothing, unfortunately, remained in the end. "I didn't care for any of them," she explained, "so I don't have one anymore." Apfel later took her mother's surname, Barrel, as a faux middle initial, despite not having a genuine middle name.

Matisse is a source of color inspiration for Iris Apfel.

It's nearly impossible to think about Iris Apfel without conjuring up images of vivid and strong hues; after all, she's not one for monochromatic ensembles. Her fondness for brilliant hues stems from her admiration of artistic expression, notably Henri Matisse, as Apfel noted. "I suppose our friend impacted everyone who dealt with [color]," she remarked. "Mr. Matisse has a knack for carving through [color]."

"The Snail," one of Apfel's favorite Matisse works, prompted her to create a vibrant ensemble consisting of a Dior cape and bracelets. Her work was also influenced by his artwork "The Horse, the Rider, and the Clown." Even at a look, the connections between Apfel and Matisse are obvious — after all, Apfel adores color. "I can't survive with color... Color can revive the dead!" she exclaimed. Whenever it comes to lifestyle or style, she has rarely sought to disguise her maturity.

Many women nowadays are concerned about maturing. Many people feel the need to conceal their age as they become elderly. Iris Apfel believes that maturing is nothing to be embarrassed about. This concept, she told CNBC, includes accepting herself as she is. She stated, "There's nothing improper with lines on your face." "Trying to seem decades youthful when you're aged is silly, and you're not deceiving nobody." As a result, Apfel has never contemplated undergoing facial surgery or cosmetic procedural treatments.

Apfel told Harper's Bazaar in another conversation that as she approached 100, she was even keener to acknowledge her exact age. "As at this time, Apfel was

96. thus, she said at 96, I believe you ought to be grateful for these additional years," she remarked. That means Apfel can wear whatever she likes, provided it's suitable. "If I can pull it off, I usually use the same outfits I used to," she added, referring to an outfit she purchased on her first date with her deceased hubby, Carl. I admire Apfel's attitude to maturing, which is grounded on good judgment, and optimism.

Carl, Iris Apfel's long-term partner, was her staunchest admirer.

From 1948 through 2015, Iris and her companion, Carl Apfel, were married and from thence had her back. Carl was a source of stability for Iris over all of these years. Initially, they worked together as co-owners of Old-World Weavers, a clothing company that specializes in vintage materials.

He remained her main supporter afterward.

According to her book, "We did practically this all together," Iris Apfel said following his death in 2015, according to CNBC. This book would not have been possible without his enthusiasm and unfailing commitment." Carl, she added, was the one who inspired me to pursue stardom. "The compliments I earned gave him far more pleasure than they gave me," she wrote.

Carl was definitely a significant role in Iris' existence. And so, it's obvious to understand why his demise would have been such a shock to Iris after so many years of being married.

Duke Ellington's companion, the fashion icon, was a musical superstar.

Iris Apfel formed a connection with Duke Ellington, amongst the most popular jazz musicians in the world, while still in design school. She was a major fan of jazz music and had been working on a paper about Duke Ellington, she told The Telegraph. She summoned the confidence to approach him at the stage door when he arrived in town for a concert. She remembered, "I got all dressed up; I guess I had more nerve than brains."

You shouldn't live in the past. Live in the moment. The past is gone, and there's no way to get it again. It was terrible; it's over; move on to another blunder.

Blunders are not deliberate actions. 'You only have one journey, baby, so adore it,' my spouse used to remark this constantly.

"I had a wonderful 68-year marriage. Carl passed away three days into his 101st anniversary in 2015. I was initially devastated. I didn't imagine I'd be able to handle it, but I understood that he was like a stage mom and wouldn't want me to sit home and wallow in self-pity. He truly pushed me. I had possibilities that I assumed he would dismiss with an 'Oh, forget it.' 'No, do it,' he'd say. 'You must do it. Go for it.

A colleague of the musical group came to answer the door and complimented her on her attire, indicating that Apfel was looking fantastic with her style of fashion even back then. "When I described my goal, he assured me that the Duke would see me." She and Ellington actually met and were instant buddies. To her mother's chagrin, he even took her to Chicago to meet other prominent jazz artists.

Iris Apfel documentary

Albert Maysles, a well-known documentary filmmaker, picked Iris Apfel as the subject of his upcoming project in 2016. The documentary, simply named "Iris," gives an insight into her life and career. Maysles learned about Apfel's teaching program at the University of Texas after hearing about it through Vogue.

Apfel initially rejected the concept. Her companion ultimately persuaded her that it was too fantastic a chance to pass up.

Being the subject of such a well-known video was both exhilarating and sensational for Apfel. "I'm quite delighted by the feedback we're receiving," she told The Cut, "Since I had no idea what was coming; I assumed people might simply chuckle, you know, in an inappropriate way." Apfel also appreciated that the film depicted her as much more than "an empty-headed socialite."

Iris Apfel's favorite food?

Iris Apfel has very precise culinary preferences. She's tried almost every dish you can conceive of, she told Healthyish. "My husband and I used to be quite daring while we were younger," she remarked. Her preferences seem to be somewhat calmer as she has grown older.

For lunchtime, she normally consumes white fish or lean beef with veggies, accompanied by fruits. She is particular about the grade of red meat she consumes. She stated, "I seldom buy minced hamburgers and beef." "Every time we acquire a nice steak, we pound it at our residence."

Apart from introducing turmeric into her diet, Apfel does not believe in nutrition recommendations. "I believe they're definitely cuckoo," she concluded. Instead, her definition of good nutrition is straightforward: no junk food, a little salt, and no drinks. Thus, her basic, nutritious diet is clearly working for her!

8

Iris Apfel's life lessons

I ris Apfel's full factorial design didn't put much emphasis on her lifestyle, which she didn't enjoy. She approached life with an intellectual mindset. She'd remind all she had met; that they can't have everything at once.

"When I was approximately ten years old, my mother had decided to return to work, which was disastrous for me, a child growing up. For me, I took as my mother seemed to have abandoned me. As a result, I decided that if I eventually get married someday and pursue a career, I may never have kids. Because I wouldn't want my kids to experience all I went through when my mom went back to work. So, you can't have it all, and our world is filled with decisions."

Do not waste time regretting it

"You're going to be a disaster if you make a court case out of everything." Once an individual is motivated and inspired, they have a better probability of success in any endeavor. People have been found to offer their best when these elements are present.

Even professionals can attain their objectives with the support of inspiration. Two of the most important keys to effective decent human beings are motivation and enthusiasm.

Both tangible and non-physical objects can provide motivation and encouragement to a person. Encourage them with great achievements. When an individual is emotionally discouraged, they require motivation and encouragement. This person will lose the ability to see the bright side and will retreat to self-pity once not motivated.

Parents and neighbors can lead to significant improvements with encouraging and supportive words. Religious institutions can also provide motivation, which will undoubtedly assist you in getting your life back on track.

Enthusiasm and inspiration are unusual qualities in today's environment. People are increasingly losing their desire to improve their lives.

By helping us to exceed our daily experiences and constraints, inspiration allows us to see novel opportunities. Inspiration affects our perceptions of our own talents and moves us from indifference to potential. Because of its elusive character, inspiration is sometimes neglected.

Its tradition of being considered miraculous or extraordinary hasn't improved the situation. Inspirations can be triggered, caught, and influenced, and it has a significant impact on key life outcomes.

It's always fashionable to be oneself.

"It's in your blood. Fashion is something that can be learned, much like being stylish and having an excellent style. It's all a crucial factor to consider. It's how you see things, how you think about them, and how you portray yourself. And the greatest way to achieve it is to be yourself rather than trying to be someone else. I'm not going to advise you on how to be stylish. I'm not sure why today's young folks desire to appear the same. It makes me so unhappy.

I believe they are missing out on a lot. Your uniqueness is really valuable. "Your lines on your face are quite normal. There is nothing awry."

Wrinkles are a mark of bravery for me. Why attempt to conceal it if God is gracious to you and grants you all those years? Why do that? Plastic surgery is something I don't agree with unless you've been in a disaster or were born with a nose like Pinocchio, which God forbid. Otherwise, what's the point of being nipped and tucked? It's ridiculous because it makes you seem squeezed after a while, and no one will think you're 27 if you're 72. It's impossible to make your hands look younger. What's the deal with grey hair? Folks who were purported to be my pals used to remark things like, 'Why don't you go hair color?' My spouse, thankfully, enjoyed white hair, so I never colored it."

Again, Apfel never considers status, which can be a significant benefit to long life and is also a major key to her lifetime of a happy existence. Age is simply a number to Apfel, a fleeting idea. Rather than obsessing about life and death, you can focus on your profession. You'll experience joy without seeking it if you love what you do and immerse yourself in the process.

We might not always enjoy becoming old, but what do you have to lose? Accept it since it is a fact. Recognize your surroundings and make the most of your rich adventure.

Also, don't be hesitant to seek assistance.

Iris Apfel recommends thinking like a teenager to stay relevant in heart and emotions. You're drawing from the fountain of existence if you're amazed by the universe surrounding you, laughing, and wondering. These characteristics make you childlike, yet people who are youthful at heart are always looking younger. You'll be more receptive to new individuals and eager for this excitement this way.

And this is the sole reason why your age is simply a number – one of a dozen thoughts that motivate you to accomplish everything fascinating.

9

Career highlights of Iris Apfel

Apfel started as a copywriter for Women's Wear Daily and interior decorator Elinor Johnson as a young lady, decorating residences for auction and refining her flair for discovering unusual items. She also worked for designer Robert Goodman as an apprentice.

She married Carl Apfel on February 22, 1948. They founded the textile company Old World Weavers shortly afterward, in 1950, and managed it until their retirement in 1992.

The Apfel's specialized in fabric replicas from the 17th, 18th, and 19th centuries, and they traveled to Europe twice a year to find textiles they couldn't get in the US. 115 East 57th Street in Manhattan was the location of the company's New York showroom. Iris Apfel worked on several design restoration projects during her career, including work for nine presidents: Harry S. Truman, Dwight D. Eisenhower, John F. Kennedy, Lyndon B. Johnson, Richard Nixon, Gerald Ford, Jimmy Carter, Ronald Reagan, and Bill Clinton.

She thought the White House contract to be one of the easiest of Old-World Weaver's clients to work with because they mostly wanted to duplicate what was already in place. Jacqueline Kennedy was the one exception, according to Apfel. "She hired a very prominent Parisian designer to gussy up the house and make it a genuine Frenchie," Apfel said, "and the design community went crazy." After that, we had to toss everything out and start over. Mrs. Nixon, on the other hand, I liked. She was stunning.

The pair began traveling all over the world as a result of their business, and Apfel purchased non-Western handcrafted clothing.

She donned these outfits to high-society parties hosted by her clientele.

Iris Apfel joined the University of Texas at Austin's Division of Textiles and Apparel as a visiting professor in 2011.

She was the face of the Australian brand Blue Illusion and appeared in a television commercial for the French automobile DS 3 in 2016. Apfel signed a cooperation agreement with Wise Wear, an efficient innovative, on a forthcoming collection of Smart Jewelry in March 2016. Iris Apfel: Accidental Icon, a HarperCollins memoir, was published in 2018.

She signed a development modeling deal with the worldwide organization IMG in 2019 at the age of 97. Tommy Hilfiger pushed her to contract professional employment after she was constantly singled out for presentations.

Apfel traveled all over the globe with her husband Carl, purchasing fabrics for their firm Old-World Weavers, which they ran jointly if they both decided to withdraw in 1992 before becoming the world's oldest trendsetter. Her impeccable expertise led to her being recruited as an interior decorator for the White House, probably

America's most renowned residence, where she collaborated on new and redesigns under nine presidential candidates, from Harold Truman (1945-1953) through Bill Clinton (1993-2001).

The Costume Institute at the Metropolitan Museum of Art in New York opened Rara Avis (Rare Bird): The Irreverent Iris Apfel, an exhibition about Iris Apfel's style, on September 13, 2005. The exhibition's prominence spurred a touring counterpart at the Weston Museum of Art in West Palm, Florida, the Nassau County Museum of Art in Roslyn Harbor, New York, and subsequently toward the Peabody Essex Museum in Salem, Massachusetts.

Apfel's garments, decorations, and interiors will be featured in a unique exhibition at the Museum of Lifestyle & Fashion History in Boynton Beach, Florida.

10

Awards and achievements

Iris Apfel is an entrepreneur, interior designer, and fashion icon from the United States. She has established herself as one of the most influential individuals in the fashion business throughout the years. She's noted for her outgoing personality and eccentric flair.

On June 7, 2016, Iris Apfel received the Women Together Special Award for Achievement at the United Nations Office in New York during the 12th Annual Women Together Ceremony. Women Together's president and founder are Joana Caparrós Masip. Other recipients in attendance were American star Rosario Dawson, the Punta Cana Foundation, the Loewe Foundation, and several more. Malu Edwards Hurley, a committee member of Women Together and the show's MC, was awarded jointly to Iris Apfel, who was joined by Carlos Jimenez, Spain's ambassador at the United Nations Headquarters in Brussels.

In the same year, she was honored at the United Nations with the Women's Entrepreneurship Day Pioneer Medal for her commitment to the fashion business. The New Jewish Home's Eight Over Eighty Gala was awarded to her in 2017.

Iris Apfel, the industrial decorator and style icon, has been designated the winner of the Andrée Putman Lifetime Achievement Award, which she received receive on the day of her 100th birthday anniversary on August 29, 2021. In its third anniversary, the accolade honors Apfel's unique vision and eclectic trajectory as she tries to maintain the spirit of the times. This is the biggest compliment bestowed by The Créateurs Design Awards, which honor the global highest designers and inventors who are driving fashion ahead.

She complements former Nobel prize winners such as American artist, philosopher, and philosopher Robert A.M. Stern and French creative director Pierre-Yves

Rochon, who was recommended by an international council of over 200 eminent artists and designers. In January 2022, precisely around Paris Design Week, Apfel was honored at The Créateurs Awards Ceremony.

Iris Apfel made a lot of money through her design restoration efforts, which comprised nine years of the construction contract with the White House. Her presentations and galleries have also helped her financially.

Her tremendously lauded presentation at the National Museum of Art's Costume Institute is still renowned in the world of style. She began making a lot of money from her employment as a visiting professor at the University of Texas in 2011.

Albert Maysles did a video known as Iris, it was all about Iris Apfel, which was released in 2014. Commercials, product collaborations, and collaborations have all helped her make money. In 2016, she appeared in a television commercial for the French vehicle DS 3.

The symbol also became the face of Blue Fantasy, an Australian women's fashion business. Iris Apfel: Inadvertent Icon, her autobiographical, was released by Harper Collins in 2018.

She has also signed a cooperation agreement with Wise Wear, a telecommunications business, and plans to develop a Smart Jewelry collection in the coming future. She considered joining the worldwide modeling agency IMG at the age of 97.

In 2021's COVID-induced depression, she induces individuality into her clothing and wider culture, her New York home—which is a wonderful remedy for trying to fend off fashionable dissatisfaction and insufficient understanding.

The honoree's everlasting significance is echoed by Yuri Xavier, cofounder of The Créateurs Design Awards. "In a profession filled with dynamic individuals, Iris's influence spans her body of work," he continues, "causing her to become a pop-cultural phenomenon and an important personality in the world of fashion and design."

At the age of 90, Iris Apfel became the image of MAC Cosmetics in vibrant red lipstick, challenging the conventional ideas of fashion and style. "Through her lively playfulness and impeccable sense, Apfel has devoted her lifelong encouraging radical evolution in the clothing business." These awards celebrate TOMMY HILFIGER's initiatives, throughout its international accessible fashion line, to make dressing more enjoyable for those with impairments."

11

Iris Apfel's glasses

Iris Apfel, a fashion queen, famed for her enormous, round glasses, picked the collection from Zenni's bright, printed designs herself.

"I enjoy accessories, and I believe spectacles can completely make an ensemble," she remarked of the eyewear collection.

They were gathered long before I needed them. Glasses inspire or complete all of my looks for me.

We shouldn't all desire to appear the very identical, and eyeglasses are an excellent opportunity to develop your distinct flair and mix things up a bit."

She's been dubbed a "geriatric starlet." So, she says: "When I'm old, I'll dress purple," but "when I'm middle-aged, I'll channel my strength and courage and wear glasses by Iris Apfel," the 92-year-old interior decorator and fashion icon instantly identifiable by her enormous, round colored framed glasses and layers of magnificent jewelry." In 2005, the Metropolitan Museum of Art honored Apfel with a show called Rara Avis: The Acerbic Iris Apfel, which focused on her personal belongings and personality.

Eye bobs, a Minnesota-based eyeglass brand known for their creative and occasionally weird glasses, has decided to join with Apfel to develop an exceptional sunglasses line, which includes both sun reader's attention and protected combinations in a variety of distinctive styles fit for the woman herself.

So, every frame costs $99 through $125 and comes with a customized microfiber dusting and protective container made by Apfel. They may be acquired domestically at Oska near downtown Seattle.

Iris loves accessorizing and believes that spectacles can greatly affect an appearance and attire. She saves them for when she needs them. She explained, "Glasses influence or complete all of my outfits for me." We shouldn't all want to appear the same, and eyeglasses are an excellent opportunity to develop your style and mix things up."

She has an eyeglasses series called the "Iris Apfel Edition," which contains five different models. "Enjoy living Colorfully," a range of eye-catching designs such as floral print cat-eye spectacles, black-and-white polka-dot frames, and a geometric-shaped turquoise style, is part of the collection. There's also the "Bazaar Treasures" classification, which was influenced by Apfel's fondness for thrift stores, the "Signature Fashion" collection, which features enormous designs, and the "Structural Design" collection which was influenced by Apfel's enthusiasm for design. Apfel's collection features a children's line called "Mini Iris."

She emphasizes that everyone ought to make an impression. As a result, she explains, my assortment is for everyone who tries to be a little distinct — but this should be every one of us. "I'm a big fan of huge lenses, and Zenni has a lot of them." obviously, I won't walk off from using my fav color combinations, red and turquoise, for both eyeglasses and frame."

The cooperation is part of Apfel and Zenni's decade-long collaboration. Apfel is also working on an exclusive new collection for her birthday this month, as well as eyewear drops every year until 2024.

The Zenni collaboration is Apfel's most recent initiative after nearly seven decades as a powerful figure in the fashion business. Last year, Apfel donated proceeds from an autobiographical coloring book depicting various periods of her career to the University of Texas in Austin's UT in NYC program, which she founded a decade ago.

"I usually say I slipped into this job by accident, but it's good to be admired," Apfel said of her status as a fashion star. "Everyone should feel free to express themselves and have pleasure while doing so." That's something I've always strived to achieve."

12

What drew Iris Apfel to the field of design?

Fashion has always piqued my interest. My mother was quite trendy as a youngster, and I was constantly around designers, so I believe I was fascinated by design even before I was born.

Her image as a feminist icon in fashion took off from there. She wasn't done yet! She received a modeling partnership with IMG even at the age of 98, defying all previous female supermodel norms. A few days before her 100th birthday anniversary, she even launched her eyewear collection! From interior decoration to redefining modeling, to her colorful and show-stopping aesthetic, to simply living a full life, she has done it all.

As a child, I recall going shopping with my mother. She'd always provide the same piece of advice: "choose something that goes with everything!" For many years, there has been a misconception that neutral solids complement more with colors and styles.

My mother isn't alone. Many people wear nearly exclusively neutrals, not because they dislike color or design, but because they are afraid of being judged. That's very understandable! Neutrals are simple to work with.

Are they, nevertheless, satisfying? Iris Apfel proves that there are a plethora of dramatic color and pattern combinations that look stunning when combined. They're less popular since jumping into so much color and design might be scary, but perhaps that's what makes them so great. So, to people who are hesitant to add more patterns and colors into their lives, Iris advises them to go for it!

You can do it if you believe in yourself and don't let people discourage you. "You don't have to think like everyone else if you don't dress like everyone else."

Iris Apfel shows us that, instead of erring on the side of caution when it comes to your clothes, you should go big or go home! She'd probably say it the same way.

She's the perfect example of delving deep into colors and patterns and demonstrating that, in her situation, more is better. "Color can resurrect the dead," she did say after all. Bold patterns and colors, like those worn by Iris Apfel, are startling, utterly show-stopping, and accomplish far more than any mix of neutrals.

Whatever I'm doing at the time is my favorite; I try to live in the now and enjoy what I'm doing. Working at the White House was fantastic, but there were many other worthwhile endeavors as well.

Iris Apfel began her career as an interior designer with a passion for fashion. When her notable clothing was featured in a Met exhibition, she became even more famous.

So, go all out! The trick is to be deliberate and decisive. The Iris Apfel impression cannot be achieved with a half-hearted effort.

Why choose a neutral that fits with everything when you can go for a wild, wacky combination, says Apfel? And who says many patterns can't work together beautifully?

Rather than sticking to black because it goes with everything, try experimenting with other colors. Sometimes the most unlikely combinations work best.

She would suggest that when it comes to unusual combinations, don't be afraid to blend high and low fashions. Iris Apfel was known for merging designer labels with flea market finds, as well as patterns, colors, and materials from many eras.

She made a conscious effort to break all boundaries and traditions with her diverse combination. "Learn the rules so you can break them," isn't there a saying?

13

Iris Apfel wealth

Iris Apfel's net worth is unconfirmed. Iris Apfel, the fashionable legend, is certainly as dazzling and delightful as always. She enjoys her career in the fashion sector while also evidenced by her presence in life. Iris Apfel is an American entrepreneur, design professional, and style star, according to what we've been reading thus far. She has distinguished herself as one of the greatest influential individuals in the fashion business throughout the years. She is well-known for her eccentric aesthetic and outgoing nature.

She received the Women Together Special Achievement of the Year at the 12th Anniversary of the Women Together Gala at the United Nations Headquarters in New York City in 2016, and she is generally regarded as an influence on the modern fashion and model generation.

In the same year, she was honored at the United Nations with the Women's Entrepreneurship Day Pioneer Award for her contributions to the modeling industry. The New Jewish Home's Eight Over Eighty Gala celebrated her in 2017, likewise.

Iris Apfel has a personal fortune of around $25 million, as reported by Celebrity Net Worth. Her commercial companies and creative initiatives constitute the preponderance of her revenues over a seven-decade career.

She started her professional career at Women's Wear Daily before launching her textile company with her husband, Carl Apfel. The textile company Old World Weavers became quite famous and lasted from 1950 to 1992.

Iris Apfel made a lot of money from her creative restoration efforts, which included nine years of the construction contract with the White House. Her presentations and exhibitions have also helped her financially.

Her tremendously lauded exhibition at the National Gallery of Art's Costume Institute is still renowned in the modeling world. She began making a lot of money from her employment as a guest lecturer at the University of Texas in 2011.

Albert Maysles' documentary Iris, about Iris Apfel, was released in 2014. Commercials, product collaborations, and sponsorships have all helped her make money. In 2016, she appeared in a tv advertisement for the French vehicle DS 3.

The symbol then became the symbol of Blue Illusion, an item in the Australian clothing and accessories business. Iris Apfel: Inadvertent Icon, her memoirs, was released by Harper Collins in 2018.

14

Internet-based shopping

Iris Apfel, a fashion queen, believes you have no idea how and where to go shopping.

Apfel proceeds about her days with drive and zeal in the documentary. Her inability to relax seemed to delight and bothered her nephew at the same time. She is eager to spot out that getting up in the morning at her age is difficult, but she does it nevertheless, feeling that life has no meaning the minute she ceases interacting with the globe with her beauty, humor, and sincerity. In the film, she steals a line from a family friend and adds, "All I have double of hurts." A few hours in a flea market, on the other hand, are greater medication than anything in an infant container.

In an interview with The Washington Post, she said, "The hurry and bustling, it's like a punch."

Apfel resembles a combination betwixt peacock and an owl in reality. She has a plume of white tresses, a slim figure, and is taller than typical. She usually put on a style of spherical, black-framed spectacles with a saucer-shaped lens. She wears combinations of bright colors that range from fashionable slacks to monastic costumes, and she accessorizes with layers of thick bangles and necklaces that could be made of tiny pin-prick golden pearls or golfing ball ornaments.

Everything is worn with a confident nonchalance — a carriage that says, "Of course." This has always been Apfel's signature style.

"I'm the very exact basic personality I was seven decades ago," Apfel says, her Queens British accent evident as she takes a succession of telephone calls for the film's promotion. "I have the very exact basic flavor."

One may contend that fashion has warmed up to Apfel's embracing of uniqueness. But it's also evident that her aesthetic has more significance and power as she gets older. She is enthralled by beauty and unwilling to be put to pasture by it. For elderly ladies, fashion provides a variety of problems, yet Iris Apfel always comes out on top.

It isn't simple. Take, for example, one of the most popular topics in the glossy magazine world: "How to Dress for Your Age." It usually provides beneficial fashion advice for women in their 20s, 30s, and beyond, up to and including their 60s. Perhaps even a reference to the 1970s will be made. But then there was nothing even though a white American woman's typical life duration is well into her 80s.

When it comes to having a fashionable life after 60, Apfel adds, "You're meant to fade into oblivion." "By ignoring the 60- to 80-year-old demographic, the clothing companies have done themselves in. They have the time and the means to do so. They have a desire to go exploring.

"Fashion has this passion for the young ones," adds Apfel. "However, 70-year-old females do not have the physique of 18-year-olds, and 18-year-olds do not have the money of 70-year-olds."

It's difficult not to admire Apfel for resisting to be forgotten, for resisting to be forced out of style. And she may be had an impact. Fashion has praised (a few) older women in her wake. Alexis Bittar, a jewelry designer, cast Joan Collins in an ad campaign a few years ago. His new commercials feature Apfel herself.

Céline recently advertised writer Joan Didion, who is 80 years old. Joni Mitchell, 71, was used by Saint Laurent. Pat Cleveland, Bethann Hardison, and Stephanie Seymour, among others, were recently cast in Barneys New York's "Better Than Ever" ad.

Apfel's love for vibrancy, dimension, and ornamentation was sparked by her fashionable mom and nourished by a distinguished and successful professional in interior decorating, which included co-founding Old World Weavers with her spouse, Carl, which concentrated on modern reproductions of historical fabrics. "You learn a lot about people's lives," Apfel says of her overseas journeys, looking for ideas in street markets and market stalls. She claims, "It's not simply dead commodities." "It has a soul," says the narrator.

Online buying, according to Apfel, is demeaning. "I love to feel it and sense it." "Everything has vanished into the internet," she continues. "But I suppose folks seem to prefer it since it's simple and time-saving." "What do they do with all the time they're attempting to just save?" you might wonder.

Isn't it good enough to justify our time to learn about various civilizations, assess human psychology, and define ourselves?

The documentary spends a lot of time talking about design and innovation, as well as Apfel's particular way of expressing both. And she'll gladly offer assistance in assisting some befuddled young woman in balancing her interpersonal eccentricities with a corporate life that requires greater restraint. Apfel says that you won't be able to locate yourself in style. It's a collaboration, and "you have to know who you are before you can know who you are."

Apfel's greatest compelling message, though, is about inquiry. That not only supports her aesthetics but also maintains her intrigued. She is frustrated by the absence of it, particularly among the young. When she speaks to youngsters, she attempts to highlight the importance of inquiry — and the Internet isn't one of them. "The college people are not receiving sufficient instruction. Or they're just plain ridiculous. They've been damaged by the technology. "Enthusiasm is equated with hitting a trigger," explains Apfel. "I was immersed in the process of acquiring the solution [to a question] when I was a kid." That is something they do not comprehend. I believe that high-tech for early childhood is destroying them. They've been deprived of their creativity."

Despite the focus on Apfel's lavish clothing and jewels, "Iris" remains sparse and austere. There are times when Apfel is quiet, and the camera focuses on her expression. Her visage flashes with a thousand conflicting sensations. Maysles doesn't come in too close in a flashy and over-wrought style.

There's no need for a close-up. Iris Apfel isn't one for wearing a full face of cosmetics. She refuses to have cosmetic surgery. Her anxieties and mortality, as well as the pleasures and sufferings of her existence, are inscribed on her countenance. Her clothing holds all of her trips and experiences. "Iris" isn't just a picture about a woman's exceptional outer appearance; it's also an intriguing film about a rich and highly rewarding life lived by regular women.

15

Conclusion

One such great example to follow. She is an incredible source of inspiration for fashion enthusiasts and designers of all ages. She also enjoys having fashion flexibility. She'd argue that one bracelet is insufficient. There should be at least a handful of them, and they should catch the human eye. One bracelet is uninteresting. More is better, say ten at a time, on both arms and neck. Also, your spectacles should be eye-catching. Allow your attire to be unrestricted but flexible, and you should be willing to wear it after the event, even if it's your wedding gown, because it's not only for that evening or day.

Someone like the extraordinary septuagenarian, Iris Apfel, is not shy about wearing ostentatious clothing and wearing eye-catching lipstick. Her hair is a bright grey color, and she wears vibrant red, magenta, or pink lipstick.

Her Instagram profile has almost 1.7 million views and followers, earning her the title of "world's oldest teenage girl." "I don't have any restrictions because I'd just violate them, so it's a waste of money and time," she said.

That was her proven strategy for success from the beginning up until now.

She exudes intelligence as well as a good sense of appreciation.

Apfel continues to look for the perfect accessories in high-end stores, flea markets, and thrift stores until this day. She mixes products and colors that no one else would imagine merging, such as haute couture and rubbish, as well as intricate designs that are ostensibly incompatible.

When Apfel styles all simultaneously, they create a harmonious effect. That is her wonderful skill and eagle eyes for color. She simply takes risks and does not embrace the crowd. She does it herself alternatively. This is exactly the point. Don't try it. Simply be yourself.

Whenever she arrives, whether at a gallery inauguration or a fashion event, young fashion designers crowd around her.

Apfel's collections are presented with a sense of humor as well as meticulousness. Before a model walks the runway, she'll typically add the finishing touch to their appearance, such as an extra bracelet.

She instills in you the values of hard work, resilience, devotion, and tenacity in anything you do. Apfel has no intention of retiring anytime soon. Even at the age of 100, Apfel has no intention of retiring from important work. She is still working as an industrial decorator and creating a series of concepts for Lowe's, a US home renovation retailer, even when celebrating her 100th anniversary.

She's also working on new spectacles for her eyeglasses line, which includes prescription glasses with attractively striking frames, of course. "More is more, and less is boring," she explains.

I laughed out loud as I read these quotes.

Iris certainly did not advise us not to marry or have children; we make our own decisions. She created her world by the decisions she took due to the nature of her career. Carl, her husband, consented to it. Children are lovely things, and if you read this book carefully, you'll discover that Iris Apfel explains why she chose not to raise children.

You can also create your own choices and world. Allow no societal coercion; they do not live your life for you.

We don't go a day without having to make decisions. Some decisions are instinctive and don't require much consideration. People do not concentrate on decisions like what to wear, what to have for lunchtime, or which route to take to work because they are not life-altering.

Although some individuals would consider these "no-brainers," persons who tend to over-think every facet of their lives may find it challenging to make those choices. The life choice process tends to overpower these people.

As we become older, making choices becomes more difficult, and the consequences of our actions become more severe. When decisions get more complex, we begin to feel the consequences of those made on our behalf. Making decisions that influence the health and well-being of another person can cause a great deal of worry and anxiety.

Not only do we have to make these choices, but we also have to be responsible for the results and the consequences of those actions. Thus, Iris Apfel shows us that Fashion is simply the way we wear and style ourselves. However, it has several extremely significant elements, such as trends, fads, buzz, and glamour. Fashion is a global phenomenon with cultural and religious roots.

Fashion is significant, and it is the essence of who we are. For us, fashion is defined by how we feel about ourselves and the objects around us. Fashion's significance in society is divided into several strata and tiers because everyone has distinct feelings about what they wear and how they dress.

Apfel was also stylish and classy, and she outlasted various fashions. She demonstrates that fashion is more than just wearing luxury clothes, carrying the most valuable jewelry, and applying high-end makeup. It is an absolute term, implying that everyone has a different perspective on fashion. And how you hold yourself, the elegance and refinement that go into making you who you are all contribute to how you define fashion.

Fashion is significant because it not only makes you look nice, but it is also an expression of art and self in the most exotic and captivating manner.

Iris Apfel, the renowned centenarian, hasn't ceased operations and was ready to discuss her current collaboration with the Swedish clothes firm.

In clothes, interior decorating, entertainment, and everything in between, the fashion icon relishes every option to show her bright and vivid point of view.

You must first determine who you are and then seek to improve yourself. Style is all about attitude, perception, and disposition, but having an attitude requires uniqueness. We can't be like everyone else and do exactly what they're doing.

You must know who you are and stay true to it—not changing your mind every three seconds. It will be challenging at first, but it will pay off. People should value their individuality rather than wanting to fit in with the crowd.

As a result, Iris Apfel taught us not only about her love of clothing and designing but also about life overall. A rare exception to the love of fashion, her blend of textures and patterns, bright and vivid colors, and taking risks with over-the-top silhouettes are all extraordinary, as are her humor, style, and intelligence.

This final phrase from Apfel astounded me, and I found myself reading it over and over. "I'm not sure wherever my motivation comes from," she says. I'm an adventurous person who enjoys trying something different. I follow my instincts. "I just do, I improvise, too" These were her words regarding being inspired to create her collections.

"Usually, things work more often than not, and sometimes it doesn't." And it is always fascinating, though." And it's thrilling. This collection, which was released on April 14 in the United States, was sold out internationally by March 31. "I couldn't believe what I was hearing! 'Boundaries all-around corner were all sold out in 5 minutes,' people contact me each moment. Wow," she exclaims, raising her arms and applauding joyfully.

She rejoices over her victories.

www.ingramcontent.com/pod-product-compliance
Lightning Source LLC
Chambersburg PA
CBHW071333130726
47996CB00002B/740